I0057554

It's Hard to be Easy

The competitive advantages of
clearing all paths for your customers.

Diane Serbin Hopkins

Author of Unleashing the
Chief Moment Officers

Introducing the Ease Factor
Exceptional Experience Compass

net worlding
PUBLISHING

Chicago, IL
www.networlding.com

Copyright ©2021 Diane S. Hopkins
Published in the United States by
Networlding Publishing
www.networlding.com

All rights reserved.
No portion of this publication may be reproduced, stored in electronic
systems, or transmitted in any form or by any means, without written
permission from the copyright owner.

ISBN: 978-1-955750-10-3

Cover Design by Alicia Marie Zyburt

It's Hard to be Easy

The competitive advantages of clearing all paths for your customers.

Dedication & Acknowledgements

THIS IS MY FOURTH book project and like the others, the topic is something I am passionate about and I'm hopeful my research and observations will provide some Ah-Ha moments for your continued success. I'm pleased to dedicate this work to my mother, Patricia Serbin who was my "quarantine buddy", a phrase I never imagined I would use. I also offer sincere appreciation to all law enforcement and frontline caregivers who were committed to continuing their work in the face of health risks during this strange and stressful time for our world.

I am extremely grateful to my son Benjamin, my husband Robert, family, friends, mentors, and colleagues who offered their advice, guidance and enthusiasm while I wrote before and during the pandemic lockdown. As we adjusted to many sacrifices that came with staying at home, I was blessed to have this exciting project to help me keep my mind off the virus crisis… some of the time.

More specific thanks to smart colleagues who generously shared their time and views including, Dan Calista, Joseph Michelli, Griffin Eaton, and Julie Anixter.

It's hard to be easy.

The competitive advantage of clearing all paths with the Ease Factor Exceptional Experience Compass.

Dedication & Acknowledgements..*iv*

Introduction...*ix*

1: What is Ease?Exploring the
   Ease Factor Experience Compass™.....................................1

2: Why is Easy So Hard?...27

3: EASY-OLOGY:Easy Steps for an Easy Strategy...............67

4: Ease in Action..95

Summary...*117*

"Simplicity is the ultimate form of sophistication."

LEONARDO DAVINCI

CUSTOMER PATH CLEARING EXERCISES: Building Low Customer Effort Muscles:

These exercises were designed to use in groups to build awareness and understanding of the importance of customer effort and to accelerate plans for improvement.

Companies need to do the heavy lifting not the customers.

#1   What Ease Areas Need Fresh Attention?   19

#2   How Are You Training Staff to Address Ease?   20

#3   What Changes Have Been Made Disrupting Ease?   22

#4   The Happy Staff/Customer Impact Checker: 44

#5   Framing Your Easy Strategy   85

#6   How Not to Frame Customer Experiences   86

#7   Three Steps to Enhance Ease   88

#8   Customer Reaction Checklist   93

#9   Rate Your Customer Ease Culture   104

#10   Apply the Customer Effort Breeze Scale   111

Introduction

THE CLASSIC THREE DOG Night song, "Easy to be Hard" focuses on selfishness in human nature and how easy it is for people to say "No" to one another which drives cold relationships. The premise is that it's easier to be disengaged than engaged. The point of view of this book flips the words but the end result is the same. As businesses become self-centered and begin to intentionally or unintentionally ignore customer needs, the relationship goes cold and customers become disengaged. Although it is often missed in the busy-ness of business, ease is a desired and important promise all organizations must strive to deliver for their customers. Although the word "customer" is used as a general term in this book, it includes unique commercial relationships such as patient, donor, citizen, member, passenger, student, or client. And although the word "book" is used to describe the collection of papers you are reading, this work is designed to be an interactive toolbox and thought provoker for team discussions with ten exercises to accelerate authentic attention to how easy you are or are not.

The paths to improved ease apply whether you are in a Business to Consumer or Business to Business environment. This "book" is designed to help leaders in any enterprise remember the foundation of the customer relationship. The truth is the workforce and systems in any organization exist to remain relevant to and hopefully delight the customers. And being easy is a primary driver of delight.

The sales strategy for any product or service begins with having a solution or a perk that is desired for purchase and the next step is that those who may wish to buy can figure out how to make the purchase. We've all had an experience where we had to navigate too many hurdles to purchase something we wanted when we wanted it. In most cases too many hurdles can lead us to seek a competitive option and companies need to take this seriously.

I see this as a "back to basics" exploration with ease at the center of what customers deserve. There are many reasons being easy is hard and this book was written to help leaders re-imagine decisions to pursue and protect effortless experiences whenever possible.

Of course, I could not pursue a book on enhancing ease without making sure the book offered an easy experience. Here are some ease-enhancing design details for your reading pleasure:

Easy to read: with larger than normal font sizes and a great deal of relevant information packed into a book that can be digested in just a few hours.

Easy to transport: a small-sized, light-weight book that can be placed in coat pocket, computer bag or purse.

Easy to purchase: available online or directly from the author for bulk orders.

Easy to store it won't take up much space on your desk or bookshelf.

Easy to mail: if you choose to give the book as a gift to all of your staff, it fits nicely in an envelope.

Easy to apply to your work: the exercises are easy to share with your teams to help bring attention to the topic and identify pertinent paths for improvement.

Wishing you exceptionally easy customer experiences ahead!

Fondly,
Diane Serbin Hopkins

What is Ease?
*Exploring the Ease Factor
Experience Compass™*

A DIVE INTO THE value of Ease in customer care begins with the belief that what is easier is better. Since we should always be striving to be better, leaders need to constantly look for ways our people, systems or technology can enable less effort and less complexity for customers. Becoming better/easier may require offerings to be faster, slower, earlier, later, bigger, smaller, broader or tighter. These betterment paths may be opposites but can lead to an improved experience for customers with opposite desires. Offering a faster self-service checkout option may delight 75% of retail customers while 25% of customers who need personal assistance will be dissatisfied with any self-service offerings. The value of Ease depends on customer preferences and those can change day to day.

The next level exploration of Ease becomes clearer by focusing on what Ease is *not*. Whether you think about business-to-business vendor interactions or business-to-consumer experiences, customers should never face tension, frustration, delayed achievement of goals, confusion, incorrect fulfillment, or other sacrifices. Clearing the path of all possible complications for customers is the most basic definition of Ease throughout this book.

Customer Ease strategy is a focus on requiring as little effort as possible and what's acceptable customer effort depends on the customer whether an individual or company. Ways to streamline the purchase process to delight customers are best understood by thoughts we've all had when preparing to buy almost anything:

1. Allow me to engage with your company the way I prefer.

2. Proactively solve problems I am likely to encounter.
3. Be prepared to predict my actions or needs.
4. Provide options in case my actions or needs change.
5. Remember me and my needs once I've chosen you.
6. Hold my hand in some cases, leave me alone in others.
7. Fulfill your promises!
8. Strive to keep me happy so I tell others dealing with you was a BREEZE!

An exceptional customer experience in B to B or B to C offerings is difficult to achieve without some aspect of Ease and it plays an important part in all steps of a customer journey including:

Awareness – Preference – Purchase – Support - Endorsement

Reviewing these steps with teams is a good way to build better understanding of the current state of customer effort to identify possible enhancements. Here are some questions to help uncover obstacles that may be making life hard for your customers:

Awareness & Preference:

- What positive or negative perceptions are commonly held about the brand?
- How easy is it for prospective customers to find what we offer?
- How easy is it for existing customers to learn about new offerings?
- Do customers have 24-hour access for assistance with service or product details? What types of real-time access is available?
- Do we offer easy to understand value and benefit comparisons for competitive solutions?
- Is it easy to obtain information about locations, contacts, hours?

Purchase:

- If customers aren't sure what to purchase, are advisors easily accessible?
- How easy is it to find the scope or selection of services or products?
- How many payment options are available?

- Are pricing options and discounts easy to find and understand?
- Are sales staff incentivized to care for customers or just sell?
- How quickly can we fulfill orders and respond to special requests?
- Are there any restrictions on when or how purchases can begin?
- How easy is it to re-purchase?
- Are there attractive incentives for repeat purchases?
- Do clients have easily accessible training options to best leverage the solution they purchased?

Support:

- If customers are dissatisfied or service is incomplete, is it easy for customers to get answers or assistance?
- Are refunds or exchanges a hassle?
- Is support available to prepare customers to make the most of their purchase or contract?
- Are customer service teams well trained and prepared to field customer inquiries? What level of

authority do they have to quickly make something right for a customer who is dissatisfied?

• Is remote support available for those who can't visit?

• Do clients have a consistent designated contact to support their purchase?

Endorsement:

• Is it easy for satisfied customers and raving fans to share their endorsements/reviews with others online.

• Are there systems or incentives in place to encourage endorsements to support sales?

• How does the company show appreciation to customers in to sustain loyalty?

Why Ease Matters

We live in a time where instant gratification is an everyday expectation. Getting what we want, when we want it, the way we want it with little effort is a desire that's here to stay. Understanding Ease as a driver of customer satisfaction should be a gut instinct. Unfortunately, this instinct is too often forgotten or not integrated well into decision-making.

Thought leader and best-selling author, Shep Hyken made the case for why Ease matters in his book, *The Convenience Revolution* when he said, "It would be a strategic catastrophe to assume that you are already 'convenient enough' for your customer". When customers find it repeatedly difficult to interact or transact with a business, an unraveling begins that will encourage them to walk away.

Ease matters when companies fail customers as well. If like me, you believe a complaint is a gift, then making it as easy as possible for customers to complain helps create a useful stream of feedback. The gold to be mined from complaints that customers take the time to share should be valued and applied for rapid improvement. Jennifer Krippner, Vice President of the Institute for Healthcare Excellence calls this process "feedforward". As clients share what's not working for them, successful companies leverage the ability to move forward with customer complaints the guiding light.

The commonsense concept that Ease matters to customers is a hot business topic. Review of dozens of studies from various industries provided a good framework for why customer effort is a strategic imperative. Here are some sample findings:

The Filene Research Institute, a financial industry think tank reported a 15% reduction in purchase intent when customers experienced a complex transaction.

In their *State of the Connected Customer Report*, Salesforce.com published research that "70% of consumers and business buyers say connected processes are very important to win their business (such as seamless handoffs between departments and channels, or contextualized engagement based on earlier interactions)."

Premiere Contact Point, an Australian contact center consultancy studied customer service preferences and reported that, "Millennials, believe social media is an effective channel for customer service. But for social care to be effective, brands must respond quickly: **66%** of those polled expect a response within 24 hours."

Zendesk's 2019 Trends Report found that "50% of customers will switch to a competitor after one bad experience. In the case of more than one bad experience, that number snowballs to 80%." Dave Dyson,

Customer Service Evangelist at ZenDesk stated, "A great customer experience makes it effortless for customers to accomplish their goals for what they want to use your product or service for. Customer loyalty is less about big "wow" moments and more about being dependable and making things easy for customers."

Tethr, a Texas-based voice of the customer platform published results of their research on customer effort reporting that, "Only 9% of customers with easy experiences display any sort of disloyalty attitude or behavior compared to 96% of customers who have difficult experiences."

Medallia Zingle published a 2020 study about consumer post-pandemic preferences and found, "87% of consumers say they think brands should continue to offer options for things like curbside pickup that limit the need for in-person visits."

These and many other studies support new attention to reducing customer effort. Understanding the importance of Ease is the easy part. The hard work begins as organizations push to orchestrate enterprise-wide commitments to remove obstacles to Ease.

The first step is to Identify points of friction that are deliberately or inadvertently placed before customers. Friction points can exist at any point of a customer's journey and the progression can lead to the loss of business. The *Friction-Defection Progression* is something to avoid at all costs. This easy-to-use scale can help teams remember how interest can progress to defection.

Customer Interest ↘

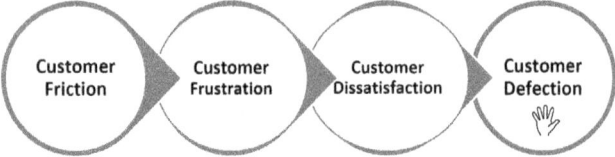

Customer Friction → Customer Frustration → Customer Dissatisfaction → Customer Defection

To further understand what Ease is and how founda-
tional it is for business success, I have developed the
Ease Factor Exceptional Experience Compass™
that further defines the important aspects of making
it easy for customers:

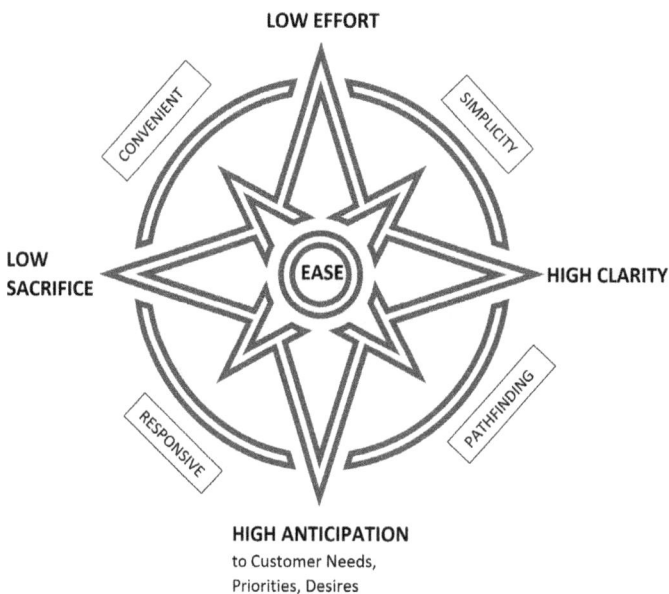

LOW EFFORT

CONVENIENT

SIMPLICITY

LOW
SACRIFICE

EASE

HIGH CLARITY

RESPONSIVE

PATHFINDING

HIGH ANTICIPATION
to Customer Needs,
Priorities, Desires

To further define aspects of an Ease Strategy, this is the **Dis-Ease Factor Compass** illustrating what can cause pain and suffering for any business. This **Dis-Ease Factor Compass** outlines **WHAT NOT TO DO!**

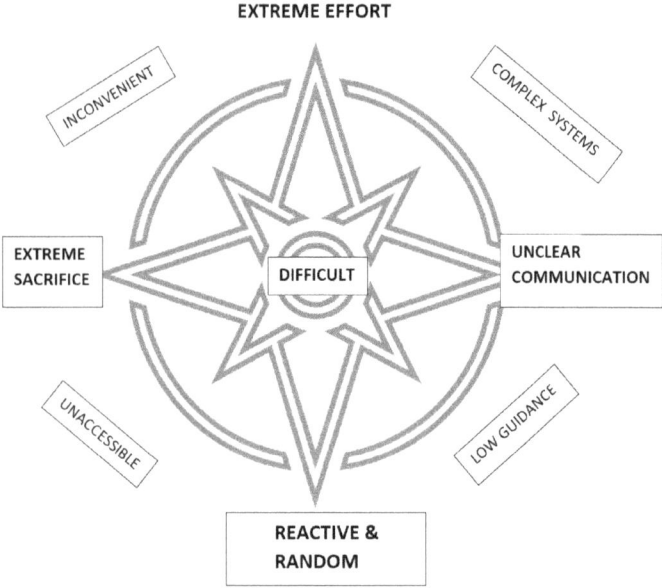

EXTREME EFFORT

INCONVENIENT

COMPLEX SYSTEMS

EXTREME SACRIFICE

DIFFICULT

UNCLEAR COMMUNICATION

UNACCESSIBLE

LOW GUIDANCE

REACTIVE & RANDOM

After years of observation and training, my definition of Ease has evolved to focus on the points of these compasses. Most of the points of compasses can apply to any business. Some points on the compass may be more important to some customers than others, so it's crucial to continually gather insights to stay up to date on changing preferences, needs and priorities.

It is common for companies to be confused about what customers or prospective customers value in desiring an easy experience. In the book, *What Customers Want*, Anthony Ulwick shares a project his team worked on with Motorola cell phone users who provided "twenty-one different ways in which customers defined easy-to-use". He shared that "ease included things such as minimizing time it took to look up a phone number and minimizing possible butt dialing." Although there are typically many obvious aspects of ease, it's important to have a detailed understanding of the customer's definitions to design desired solutions.

The reason ease needs to be a driving priority seems obvious however it can be lost in the complexity of running a business. Passion around customer ease is about preventing frustration and building positive recommendations to attract new customers. Authors, Nick Toman and Rick DeLisi conducted research with over 97,000 customers for their book, *The Effortless Experience* and found, "4 out of 5 drivers of disloyalty are about additional effort customers must put forth. Having to contact a company more than once to resolve the problem is the biggest of all". Their findings confirm the basic premise that Ease must be a core company priority and the delivery of Ease cannot be uncommon for long-term viability.

Prolific author and innovation thought leader, Tom Peters asked the question, "Where has all the friction gone?" in his book, *The Circle of Innovation*. He explored the ideas that for long-term success companies need to be "frictionless by and large". A few of Tom's predictions back in 1999 are true today. He proclaimed that "intermediaries are doomed". Think about how many industries have made life easier for customers by removing the "middlemen" and there's likely no turning back. Tom also predicted that self-service would become "more present and powerful" and self-service has certainly reduced friction for customers in so many businesses and became essential as the world adjusted to the impact of the highly contagious COVID virus.

The commitment to create effortless experiences for customers certainly suggests some obvious approaches but as with most aspirations, complicating factors exist. What on the surface seems like a friction improvement for all customers may actually be an annoyance to some. Many of us appreciate the ability to fill our cars with gas with a quick swipe of our credit card and no human interaction. Others prefer or need an attendant to come and fill the tank and despise self-serve. Two different experiences can be perceived as easy or hard by different people. Being easy isn't always easy to achieve but taking the time to understand what's relevant to specific customer groups helps avoid unintended customer dissatisfaction.

The Pandemic Effect

When defining Ease in business special attention must be given to how customer desires expanded due to the impact of the coronavirus pandemic. This dramatic change in how we all viewed our lives prompted new definitions of Ease. As businesses and customers became centered on protection from a highly conta-gious virus, there were new paths to being convenient and new tolerance for systems that were inconve-nient. Company leaders needed to identify new ways to operate while building and maintaining customer trust. Many businesses launched new consumer ad campaigns explaining how they offered "touchless" customer experiences. Curbside pick-up, e-commerce, socially distanced shopping, app ordering and delivery became the new norm and e-commerce rates have been estimated to have increased 50% during 2020. The ability to order groceries on your phone, pay for them and have someone place them in your trunk pro-vided an easy and safe shopping experience. Although inconvenient, changes such as having to stand in a que to enter a store, restricted store hours, standing 6 ft apart while waiting in line, generally became a new accepted part of shopping journeys. There are conflicting opinions on whether the pandemic effect on how consumers shop for anything will last into the future. As customer desire for safety continues to rede-fine what is most important, businesses will need to pursue easy and safe experiences. One new attempt surfaced when Nike launched a new store in New York during the pandemic to mix online ease and convenience, with a physical in-store shopping experience. Shoppers reserved a pair of sneakers online using a free app after having browsed the selection. Once style and size are set, the preferred sneakers are placed in a locker in the store, ready for the customer to show up and try on. Known as the "Speed Shop" the in-store area has lockers which can only be unlocked by the shopper's app, so they can try on shoes, and check out via the app without going near sales staff or the cash register.

Another example of post-pandemic responsiveness involves new ways customers can communicate with companies. The pandemic prompted some companies to make it easy to communicate via text for the first time. Farmers Insurance launched text messaging options to eliminate call center delays and speed up communications. The medical industry had to manage demand and patient safety by rapidly expanding the adoption of telemedicine to allow care to continue. Mental health professionals also facing high demand offered phone and video sessions and text messaging often for the first time. And all types of businesses and universities were able to stay in

business by embracing video meetings and interviews so that communications could easily continue.
These new paths to interact and transact prove that
a crisis can drive inspiration which drives innovation
and customers benefitted from new levels of Ease.

To help you apply the Ease Factor Compass the-
ories in your organization, have teams discuss the
following exercises:

🪓 Path Clearing Exercise #1:

What areas of the Exceptional Customer Experience Compass need fresh attention in your organization?

With Ease as the center of all you do, have each department list specific aspects of the customer experience that can be made easier in each of the core quadrants on the compass:

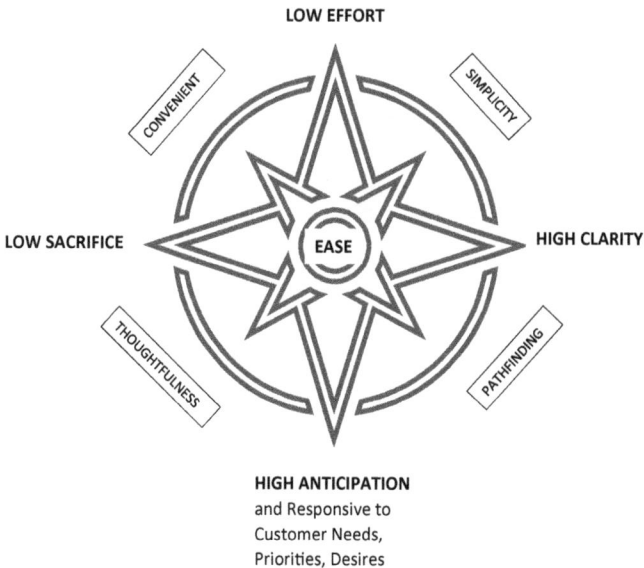

LOW EFFORT

CONVENIENT

SIMPLICITY

LOW SACRIFICE

EASE

HIGH CLARITY

THOUGHTFULNESS

PATHFINDING

HIGH ANTICIPATION
and Responsive to
Customer Needs,
Priorities, Desires

⛏ Path Clearing Exercise #2:

Dear any company in the world:

Make it easy for me to find you, understand what you offer, can offer, will offer, for me to change my mind, pay you, communicate with you, get what I want and have my needs and desires met and then it won't be easy for me to not buy from you!

Sincerely,

your potential customer, patient, donor, client, student, member, citizens

Assignment: This letter is a sample staff training exercise. Look at your current customer experience training materials or courses and see how well EASE is addressed for staff.

🚶 Path Clearing Exercise #3:

Dear Companies Wanting to Keep Existing Customers:

Your management team may know something we customers don't know but please remember that when you **CHANGE things we're used to**, our "retail muscle memory" on how to spend money with you or navigate your systems is disrupted. When you make changes to how we get what we want from you, it upsets our comfort zone.

When you completely blow up your website design and flow when we've been happily using it for 8 years and require us to "learn" a new way to give you our money, sometimes we'll need to find a path of less resistance with a competitor.

When you decide to completely redesign your store layout so we can't find what we've always been able to find, it's frustrating. It strips a happy customer of some comfort and ease. Why do that to us? Thanks for listening…

Your existing customers

Assignment: Review any changes made in operations or sales systems to see where customer habits have been disrupted.

EASE

THE MODERN SYMBOL OF EASE: The Easy Button

The story of the Easy Button has been shared in numerous publications over the years and the summary of many reports is that the "button" is a concept designed by Staples' advertising agency, McCann Erickson, for the 2005 Super Bowl. The original campaign depicted tasks that have no easy solution and each time, pushing an Easy Button saved the day. The commercials included the phrase, "Wouldn't it be nice if there was an easy button for life. Now there's one for your business. Staples. That was easy."

The company began selling actual Easy Buttons in the Fall of 2005 that said, "*That was easy*," when pressed. The buttons started at $4.99 and are now around $8.99 with the first $1 million of sales donated to Boys and Girls Clubs of America.

"Companies must constantly check to see if they are inadvertently creating paths of most resistance for their customers. If you are, there will always be a smart competitor ready to take them by the hand to a path that's easy".

DIANE SERBIN HOPKINS

"When we develop real empathy for the people we serve, our jobs start to become callings. Empathy can awaken us to the power that we have to change the course of everyday life".

DEV PATNAIK

Why is Easy So Hard?

STRUGGLES WITH VENDORS OR retailers that made it hard for any of us to be or stay a customer happen regularly. The typical reaction is feeling unimportant to the company or that they don't know what they're doing. Some customers face the frustration and carry on as a customer, others take the time to complain and offer suggestions for improvement, but many simply take their business elsewhere. I spent 18 months asking business leaders from a variety of industries what they thought caused companies to make it difficult for the people who keep their companies afloat? Merchants, government managers, hospital executives, consultants and retailers collectively had lots to say and the most frequent answer was, "stupidity". It was mentioned not as a glib response but as a serious summary of how they felt something so basic and obvious could be missed by teams who have so much at stake. This led me to want to understand more about organizational stupidity and how it contributes to why easy can be so hard. Blogger, Joe Martin published a quote that frames how some companies miss the customer ease mark, "Ignorance and stupidity are not the same. Ignorance is not knowing what to do; stupidity is not doing what you know." It would seem that all businesses should know what to do to make life easy for their customers.

I developed a new perspective around the concept of organizational stupidity after reviewing a 2015 study by Psychologists Balazs Aczel and Bence Palfi of Eotvos Lorand University in Budapest, Hungary and Zoltan Kekecs of Baylor University who led research around levels of individual stupidity. Their interviews and observations, led to a theory that there are three levels of stupidity, otherwise known as "foolish behavior".

- Confident Ignorance- the most serious level
- Lack of Control-a mid-level type of stupidity
- Absentmindedness-the lowest level[1]

If, as I found in my interviews, organizational stupidity allows difficult customer experiences to thrive, I see some lessons connecting these levels of stupidity to unintelligent creation of unnecessary effort.

Confident ignorance is a dangerous state for individuals or companies, and it is a situation where we tend to act *believing* we know the full picture. Teams that believe they know what is actually going on while they are actually detached from the day-to-day operations, are likely to be confident with their actions and ignorant about the unintended inconvenient consequences. This is commonly referred to as the "believing your own press" syndrome.

Lack of control also leads to problems for individuals and companies and in this level of customer culture stupidity are companies allowing competing priorities to overshadow the needs and desires of customers.

1 Aczel, B., Palfi, B., & Kekecs, Z. (2015). What is stupid? *Intelligence, 53*, 51-58 DOI: 10.1016/j.intell.2015.08.010

Sometimes there is a lack of control in the core business due to distractions around acquisitions, past successes, competitors, or complacency around mediocre management. Lack of control could also be a lack of effective coordination of decisions that may impact customers. If detailed customer impact is only considered once there's a complaint, that's a lack of customer-centric control.

Absentmindedness seems to be more of an unintended type of stupidity, yet the consequences are just as real. Companies that are in constant "DO mode" with little time for "THINK mode" are likely to forget or miss important customer cues that offerings are too darn hard to access. Organizations that experience widespread issues with burnout end up with a workforce that is tired, overly stressed, and not fully present. These conditions can prompt absentmindedness in all of us. It is ok to be a hard driving, aggressive, fast paced company, until the customer gets lost in the activity.

All three levels of these not so smart strategies can be addressed by a willingness to face the situation. An effective response is to thoughtfully uncover people, policies and systems that have allowed organizational stupidity to influence operations, culture, and customer satisfaction.

Consider performing an *Unintelligent Customer Effort Assessment* and look for areas where your business may be fostering:

☑ Over-confidence and customer need ignorance
☑ Lack of customer-centric focus and control
☑ Absentminded customer impact operations

Another explanation of why businesses can make life difficult for B to B or B to C customers comes from Dan Calista, founder of the consulting company Vynamic who shared his observations on Ease. Conditions he believes make easy so hard to sustain are:

- a poor culture with low employee morale translates to staff discouraging customer ease since they aren't motivated to care.

- businesses who don't know and can't identify their customers so they are hung up trying to figure out which customers to target.

- bureaucratic cultures where risk mitigation is the top priority and contracting becomes almost impossible.

The pursuit of enhanced customer effort often involves removal of unnecessary steps in the process of attracting and keeping a customer. Taking a 30-step process and turning it into 5-step process will likely delight those who were burdened by the extra 25 steps, but the improvement process can be difficult to implement. Easy is hard to provide to customers when disruptive changes are required. Internationally acclaimed abstract artist, the late Hans Hofman beautifully described the reason continual improvement is continually important when he said, "The ability to simplify means the ability to eliminate the unnecessary so that the necessary may speak." There are many reasons why organizations allow unnecessary customer effort to exist. Through my direct observations with clients and interviews with business leaders, I have crafted a model of core conditions that lead to customer experiences that are unacceptably difficult.

Leading your organization to avoiding the Paths of Most Resistance otherwise known as... The Hard Way:

> The main roads to the HARD WAY for customers intersect around a lack of well-coordinated knowledge and sharing of customer preferences at all points of contact. The old "right hand doesn't know what the left hand is doing," problem leads to companies losing sight of how to make it easy for their customers to become and remain customers.

This Way to
Tediousness &
Inconvenience

PATHS OF MOST CUSTOMER RESISTANCE™–

Companies make it hard to be easy for customers when the following conditions exist:

CULTURE

A company culture drives the framework for what's important and how strategies are designed. The foundation of why easy can be so hard is the state of company culture which dictates decision-making and what is tolerated and rewarded. To complicate things further, many organizations actually sustain multiple cultures across the enterprise based on different locations, night shift vs. day shift, etc. In some cases, a culture is not consistently customer-centric due to leader profiles that lean more toward narcissism and less toward servant leadership. If leader ego is driving culture, the company can become a reflection primarily of individual leader values and those may or may not support customer needs. This is a tricky topic to discuss, however it can be an important reason why an organization loses sight of how difficult the customer journey may be.

In the book, *Hug Your Haters*, author Jay Baer advises businesses to embrace criticism as an important way to sustain customer satisfaction. He acknowledges it's a difficult path and said, "it takes cultural alignment, resource allocation, speed, a thick skin and an unwavering belief that complaints are an opportunity". Cultural alignment around Ease can be a difficult pursuit but is required for sustainable customer delight.

Another way company culture can negatively impact Ease is when the culture is ignored or taken for granted. One of my favorite quotes about culture is from author of *Leading with Intention,* Mindy Hall, PhD who said, "Choose to intentionally shape the culture because once you witness the power of culture, it becomes the most important levers of success you will ever experience". I have seen this to be true and I have seen this absolutely impact whether customer experiences are mediocre or exceptional. To sustain an exceptional experience culture with Ease as a promise, the workforce at all levels must first under-stand that Ease is a crucial aspiration and priority. In the book, *The Culture Code*, author Daniel Coyle dis-cusses impressive culture frameworks from Gregg Popavich, former coach of the San Antonio Spurs. One driver of his success was providing the team with a "big picture perspective". This deals with the power of making sure everyone understands the larger context in which their work and influence impacts the over-all company performance. When staff are focusing primarily on their narrow contributions and focused more on operations than customers, they are more likely to make it hard for customers since customer ease gets lost. Leaders who deliberately nurture a culture for high performance must regularly remind staff about the big picture and how they connect to it. This supports a culture of customer centricity but also helps individual contributors feel important and valued which can boost a sense of ownership. To leverage the power of customer ease companies should assess how clear the expectation of being easy to do business with has been in the past. If it's been assumed, the goal may not be well understood. If Ease isn't present in the employee experience, then it may be time to set an example in how staff interact with the company. Once the desired state has been established, that expectation must be shared over and over in a memorable way. As you build a customer-centered culture with Ease at the center, the roadblocks for new customers to arrive and existing customers to stay loyal will begin to disappear.

Since operations, strategy and culture are interwoven, assessing current state strategies can clarify how customer effort goals align with operations. A study by researchers George Day and Prakash Nedungadi of the Wharton School identified three strategy types of companies across industries. They described three types of business strategies… "Self-Centered Companies (operations focus), Customer-Centered Companies and Competitor/Market Centered Companies."

Reflect upon how your organization operates and decide which of these three strategy categories fits your culture. Of course, market factors, business maturity and resource availability issues can impact these categories over time, however one key driver is usually obvious. When reviewing the likely impact to customer effort based on strategy types that drive culture, Customer-Centered Companies will embrace Ease as a priority. Companies that are more Self-Centered are likely to put the comfort of the workforce and contractors as a priority. These companies will likely put margins above mission or expense management over customer acquisition and retention and that may work in some circumstances. Companies that are Competitor/Market focused likely operate in a more reactive mode based on market forces instead of proactively planning for low customer friction.

The last aspect of culture that may interfere with Ease is an overall expectation to sustain a fast-paced environment which may be a good thing to stay ahead of competitors but may cause negative consequences and friction for customers. A fast-paced culture that rewards growth and how quickly results are pursued and achieved can be hard on staff and hard on customers. A fast-paced atmosphere can lead to the customer getting lost in the energy to build the business. When fast-pasted teams successfully drive new interest, that can lead to unexpected demand and limited supplies or team member shortages to accommodate the demand. These developments can prompt new hurdles for customers to navigate.

Since Ease can be a competitive advantage and driver of loyalty, consider what actions are needed to strengthen your company culture and strategies to be customer effort centered. It will be valuable to conduct a current state culture check to see if customer effort is being negatively impacted by the concepts described above: Leader Ego Driving Culture, Commitment to Embrace Customer Complaints, Lack of Clear Customer Effort Expectations, Driving Strategy Type and Commitment to being Fast Paced.

Deeper understanding of these influencers of culture can accelerate a direct route to clearing all paths for customers.

Staff Needs Ahead of Customer Needs:

The well-known theory that happy employees lead to happy customers has been proven over the years however, in some businesses, staff needs and desires have driven decisions that can drive customers to your competitor. Whether you look at hours of operation, preferred parking, return policies or staffing levels, companies can't achieve "easy centered-ness" if staff needs are a higher priority than customer needs. Valerie Willis, Vice President of Tom Peters Company shared her perspective on the topic, "The companies that create Ease put in processes that are easiest for the consumer vs. processes that are easiest for the organization. Those companies value the customer's time and perspective and are driven to retain each customer".

It is important to stay current on what makes employees happy and engaged, but it may be time to compare employee satisfaction efforts with the unintended impact on customers before changes are implemented. In the book, *Woo, Wow, Win*, authors Thomas Stewart and Patricia O'Connell advise companies to strive for "*Service Elegance*" where great customer experiences don't require your teams to "break a sweat". They say, "the best way to achieve that kind of elegance is to start by making things easy for customers, then work backwards to your own activities". Unfortunately, most companies start with the realities of operations and make decisions based on what's affordable, legal, and efficient and customer needs come later. Stewart and O'Connell predict that when operations and cost considerations come first, "you'll end up tying customers in knots."

Another reason why "EASY is HARD" revolves around how easy it is to overcomplicate almost anything. When staff needs trump customer needs, overcomplication of the steps customers face can become the norm. Some of the key contributors to overcomplicated offerings or systems are usually the unintended consequences of well-intended solutions.

As you pursue Ease as a core promise for customers, look to guard against some of these situations that can allow overcomplication to grow in your organization:

1. *Rampant Silos* – when there is little sharing of priorities and projects in an organization, the lack of well-integrated knowledge of what's really going on can result in overcomplicated offerings and processes. Commitments to transparency and collaboration help to reduce silos that interfere with smooth customer experiences. Without that commitment leaders may only see the damage silos cause when customers complain, leave or file suit.

2. *In with the New-In with the Old-* overcomplicated processes can result when organizations enthusiastically embrace new systems or ways to relate to customers without removing some of the old systems. The combination of old and new layers often make life more difficult for customers.

3. *Regulatory Paralysis*- All businesses must operate within regulations and although this is a required commitment, overcomplication can develop when companies go overboard with regulations driving systems and the customer is further down on the list. Identifying how to meet requirements without unnecessary steps for customers should be an ongoing priority.

🛤 Path Clearing Exercise #4:

The Happy Staff/Customer Impact Checker:

Staff Satisfaction Opportunity: Shorter Call Center Hours Customer Impact Questions:

1. Will the opportunity, if implemented likely cause any inconveniences for current or potential customers? List all.

2. What preparation would be required with staff before implementing the proposed customer satisfaction opportunity, so teams are prepared to explain any changes to customers?

3. Will the proposed opportunity make it easier for customers to do business with a competitor?

To put Customer Ease at the center of operations, consider launching new policies and procedures that will guide decision-making to minimize customer sacrifice before deciding what is an employee satisfier. Some policies to consider are:

1. Customer complaints on difficulties should require root cause analysis and response plans within 1 week of issue review.

2. New construction or new offering funding should not be approved without a comprehensive Customer Ease plan driving the shape and scope of the new offering.

3. Customer ease policy and procedure reviews as an ongoing priority to stay up to date on how consumer preferences change and how well systems within the company are aligned.

Distractions Drive Decisions

Individuals can't do their best work when they are constantly distracted, and neither can companies. Mindfulness in business applies to the importance of staying alert to how everything impacts the customer. Unfortunately, many small and large distractions can take over and when this happens things get harder and harder for customers. In the book, *Fully Present-The Science, Art and Practice* by Susan Smalley, PhD, and Diane Winston describe mindfulness as a "mental seat belt that can protect us from bumpy, twisting and turning roads in life". Companies can apply this concept to all the distractions that bombard organizations daily. If customer Ease is an organizational seatbelt that's always in place as the company moves forward, unnecessary friction and frustration will be avoided. When teams embrace a "customer ease seatbelt" it will be harder for competitors to pass you and you have a better chance of arriving safely at the desired destination of continued viability!

A distracted leadership group may lose sight of how much friction exists in the business. This situation can be driven by new regulations, rapid growth, changes in leadership or competitive pressures. Successful companies make a commitment to reasonably deal with distractions while committing to a customer need review driving decisions. Shaun Lovejoy, CEO of Courage to Lead explored this concept in his podcast, *Signs of a Distracted Leader*. He said, "Distracted leaders pursue new potential at the neglect of improving existing processes. Focused leaders are ruthlessly and boringly consistent". Consistent consideration of customer ease as part of decision-making despite the many distractions of the day is an important exceptional experience strategy.

No Accountable Customer Experience Strategy:
Whether those who buy from you are subscribers, patients, members, clients, passengers, or donors, one of the biggest reasons for customer dissatisfaction is that customer-facing staff are confused about desired behaviors. In addition, there is often little or no accountability to ensure the right things are done the right way and at the right time.

Consistent and effective preparation of frontline staff is a requirement for smooth customer experiences. Most organizations pursue customer service standards, but the standard setting can be confusing and overly complex for distracted frontline staff to follow well. In their 2010 Harvard Business Review article, *Stop Trying to Delight Your Customers*, Matthew Dixon, Karen Freeman and Nicholas Toman researched many successful customer service policies and reported, "Telling frontline reps to exceed customers' expectations is apt to yield confusion, wasted time and effort, and costly giveaways. Telling them to "make it easy" gives them a solid foundation for action".

Unfortunately, some businesses don't have to worry about having an accountable strategy since they don't have a deliberate customer experience strategy at all, especially one that's integrated with operations. The old "what gets measured matters" theory applies to customer satisfaction and needs to be well aligned in all areas. Some key questions to explore that may help frame an accountable customer experience strategy are:

1. Are the financial incentives supportive of ever-improving customer ease?

2. Are productivity metrics driving cost-savings or revenue growth while impeding attention to customer ease?

3. Does the company regularly sponsor required staff training on customer experience expectations and encourage idea sharing on ways to constantly improve?

4. Does the company have the courage to share customer complaints broadly while measuring numbers of complaints?

All industries can benefit by pursuing effortless customer experiences with the same rigor applied to recruitment, sales, and operations strategies to stay ahead of competitors. Healthcare is one industry notorious for being difficult for patients to understand and navigate. The physician referral app ZOC DOC acknowledged how complex medical care is known to be in their 2020 slogan…

"ZocDoc. Healthcare but easy".

This group acknowledged upfront the sacrifices and suffering people face when seeking inpatient and outpatient care. In 2020 Change Healthcare commissioned a study conducted by the Harris Poll called the Healthcare Consumer Experience Index to better understand how easy or hard it is to find, access and pay for services in the healthcare industry. This survey of over 1900 consumers discovered that 62% believe "the healthcare experience feels like it is purposely set to be confusing," and 2/3 said, "every step of the process in healthcare is a chore and not one aspect of healthcare was described as effortless". The study leaders concluded that "Providers who streamline the experience to meet patient expectations will gain a competitive advantage". This scenario translates to almost any industry you can imagine.

Other industries known to be difficult to engage with are covered in the Freshdesk 2019 Customer Happiness Benchmark Report. Some of the top industries known to be hard to contact or resolve issues with include: Education and Government agencies, Transportation and Telecommunications. The industries on this list do not have a reputation for implementing accountable low friction strategies that are well-integrated with operations.

Technology Investment Romance:

Many companies fall in love with technology since new tech solutions are seen as a path to reduce high overhead costs and realize competitive advantages. Attraction to the newest technology can sometimes lead to a relationship break with customers when the customer experience is not considered before implementation. One caution for those who feel technology is the answer to improving customer ease was highlighted in a salesforce.com study that found *"70% of consumers say technology has made it easier than ever to take their business elsewhere."*

Some customers are reluctant to adopt new technologies especially if they have had a long-standing pleasing relationship with a retailer. This reluctance or ineffective guidance can result in customers causing a delivery or service failure due to misuse or misunderstanding of the technology-enabled transaction. If they fail to use the technology as intended and a poor customer experience results, specialized service recovery approaches may be needed to address how they were forced into new behaviors with ineffective guidance. This situation can cause extreme frustration and should be considered when designing service recovery options.

Technology is typically designed to speed things up or simplify transactions and offer a more comprehensive transfer of necessary information. With those grand intentions, be sure that unprepared customers don't have to face steep or cumbersome learning curves to master the promised benefits from new technology. Just because a new technology is turned on doesn't mean it's a good customer solution. The ability to give customers technology enabled paths as well as human or manual paths, can position a business to meet individual needs. Chatbots work well for some interactions but when combined with a live agent when needed, the customer experience will be much less likely to be frustrating and complicated. Offering options can be complex and expensive and hard to justify once a large technology investment has been made. Whenever possible consider high and low-tech options to promote customer comfort.

In the book, *Unlocking the Customer Value Chain*, Thales S. Teixeira, shares results from his Harvard Business School research and recommends that new offerings should favor operations over technology to prove offerings work for customers first. He states, "Early on, you cannot expect technology to match human interaction sensitivity in recognizing problems with the flexibility to quickly adapt as you learn. Uber went door-to-door to get its first drivers to sign up. Airbnb did the same for its renters, and convinced people to list their homes. Only later was technology used to accelerate the process."

One of the most common examples of technology improving customer effort is self-service. Typically, a self-service option is driven by potential labor cost savings. Cost saving is not a bad thing, but just because your organization sees solid savings from self-service systems, it doesn't mean customers see it as a benefit. Self-service options whether at a bank, an amusement park, retail check-out or airline will only make life easier for your customers if the alternative is a drain (such as long lines at the airport) and if the self-service systems are intuitive and easily accessible. When self-service truly creates a much more beautiful experience for customers, you may be able to charge customers a bit more for a self-serve option.

Reduction of customer effort often drives technology investments in both B to B and B to C customer journeys. The value of this strategy was confirmed in a study conducted by the Customer Contact Council in 2010 of more than 75,000 people who had inter-acted over the phone with contact-center represen-tatives or through self-service channels such as the web, voice prompts, chat, and e-mail. A key finding, they shared was that "delighting customers doesn't build loyalty; reducing their effort—the work they must do to get their problem solved—does". Acting deliberately on this insight can help improve ser-vice, reduce service costs, and decrease customer churn. It's important to check whether any proposed technology enhancements are driven by a romantic notion that all technology is good or if the technology truly enables reduced effort and desired interactions for customers.

Technology enhancements often center around expanding the digital presence of a company that previously centered around in-person or live phone transactions with digital as a secondary channel. The Covid 19 pandemic rapidly forced many companies to transition to a primary digital platform and the impact will be long lasting. It's clear that voice-enabled shop-ping options will continue to grow to simplify customer experiences. The Center for Client Retention offers guidance on how businesses should align to reduce customer effort and founder Richard Shapiro recommends, "brands that are paying attention will invest heavily in voice commerce–literally putting their money where their (customers') mouths are."

A 2020 Digital Customer Experience Report study conducted by the CX Networks found, "brands must make it as easy as possible for users to achieve their goals and not test customer patience levels", One of the participants in the study was Lucas Robinson, CMO of Crediful who stated, "People don't have time anymore to spend hours browsing as they would much rather grab and go". Whether your company has a technology romance blooming with digital commerce, software solutions, artificial intelligence or video consultations, customer effort should be a driver of the design and implementation.

Risk Aversion Paralysis:

Safety must be a core value for staff and customers and certainly following all applicable laws in conducting business should never be optional. Unfortunately, there are situations where the fear of risk sets all direction in a company and the customer gets lost in the process. Innovative companies have no choice but to face potential risks head on and when senior executives or owners embrace continual innovation, they prepare for the potential risk as well. If the desire to mitigate all risk is more important than customer experience impact, a crippling tension can surface. Yes, trying new things is scary but that's the fuel of growth and protection of market relevance. It's crucial for companies to find a way to balance risk aversion and paths to delight customers. Some examples of how companies allow fear of risk to drive strategy are when frontline staff are not empowered to address customer issues in the moment. The fear that some-one might go too far or offer something unreasonable prevents exceptionally easy experiences from becom-ing the norm. Risk-based paralysis is also seen when a company has made investments in systems or perks that aren't delighting customers but no one has the courage to pull the plug. Think about ways fear of risk may be frightening customers away.

Risk aversion can also impact customer Ease when a company shifts decision-making to focus on cus-tomers as possible criminals. When situations arise where a company has been harmed by those who manipulate systems or outright steal, the organizational response can sometimes push to prevent further harmful activity while inadvertently making life difficult for the 99.9% of the law abiding, money-spending customers. If potential criminal behavior is driving operations, consider a review of procedures that may punish cherished customers more than they deter bad actors. If customers feel disrespected, and must navigate one complicated system after another, growth will be negatively impacted.

Business strategy expert Peter Drucker said, "Whenever you see a successful business, someone once made a courageous decision", and I certainly agree that courage is required to reliably deliver effortless experiences. Whether it be the courage to change compensation plans, to launch innovative solutions, challenge conventional wisdom or not to allow risk mitigation to leave customers feeling unimportant, ease enhancement should be a top consideration. Companies and individuals can be lulled by a sense of security around how things have always been done and avoid pushing limits. When business as usual isn't driven by a quest to be extremely easy to do business with, courageous customer leadership is needed.

Ineffective Customer Connection and Knowledge Systems:

This contributor to complicated customer interactions centers around a lack of accurate knowledge of what different customers need and value and how well the organization is aligned to accommodate those needs. Traditional and non-traditional ways to connect staff to customers can improve required effort. Harry Kraemer, the former Chairman and CEO of Baxter shares how important it was to connect teams to the customer so that each staff member could see how they related to a "greater purpose" in his book, *From Values to Action*. A key strategy he launched was to invite customers/patients to visit the manufacturing plants to affirm that jobs were more than just putting connectors on devices but about keeping people with renal failure alive. He shared the power of events where hundreds of team members heard patients share how their lives were saved due to the device they built. Deliberate efforts to keep staff connected to customers expands empathy and can offer important reinforcements for the culture. When staff members connect with the customer's plight, they are more likely to be motivated to make life easier for them.

Establishing effective customer familiarity and learning approaches allows an organization to monitor and act to not only fix an issue with one customer, but to enhance the ability to anticipate similar issues to head off future problems. Whether a company offers inconvenient hours of operation or doesn't realize how equipment failures impact customers or that service agents are not following proper protocol to resolve requests, these are examples of an ineffective customer knowledge system, a type of institutional ignorance. Although there are many robust software solutions to help companies maintain a comprehensive customer experience management strategy, not all companies have adopted or sustained these solutions. A huge source of dissatisfaction for many customers is that companies don't maintain relevant customer information that's well integrated across all departments. The ability for any area of a company to access up-to-date and comprehensive customer information will reduce potential friction points such

as delayed responses, repetitive requests for information, and broken promises. These customer insights
management systems support "extreme listening" to
customer concerns, desires, and preferences. The capture and reporting of daily or hourly customer preferences from every imaginable source, (call centers,
social media, websites, sales staff, complaints, etc.)
offers deep understanding of issues and can cure
ineffective knowledge systems syndrome.

An important aspect of knowing the customer is
the presence of organizational empathy. In his book,
Wired to Care, Dev Patnaik, CEO of Jump Associates
observes that empathy leads to growth since when
empathy is part of business decisions, teams develop
new levels of relevancy. He states, "A widespread
sense of empathy starts to influence the culture of a
place, giving it a sense of clarity and mission". When
too many other priorities begin to bury the basic
steps for customers to make purchases, companies
have lost clarity and lost sight of the true mission. The
cure may be to consider empathy as a growth strategy. If teams aren't encouraged to incorporate a sense
of empathy into all aspects of customer interactions,

that blind spot will allow customer friction which ultimately makes it hard for you to satisfy customers.

Not having effective customer knowledge systems in place is a common reason why easy can be so hard to establish and maintain. Gathering of real-time feedback from as many sources as possible and sharing that broadly with staff who have influence is often inconsistent or non-existent. Maintaining a prompt flow of customer dissatisfiers or suggestions for an improved streamlined experience helps make it easy for customers to become and stay customers. Without reliable, fresh insight gathering companies miss regular incremental and radical opportunities to remove hurdles for customers. If you can't afford an enterprise-wide customer data system, look for new ways to integrate customer feedback at every point of contact using existing systems or more frequent observations and interviews. If you are unable to mobilize daily updates, try for weekly or monthly synthesis of what customers are saying or doing. Without a timely and reliable flow of customer insights and a culture that values prompt action, your Ease strategy will be significantly limited.

In addition to digital monitoring and reporting, companies need to embrace the power and knowledge held by customer-facing staff. The diverse view of the customer held by those delivering experiences in person or on the phone is one of the most untapped resources any company has. The frontline staff see what those in the boardroom don't see and they know things leaders don't know. As covered in *Unleashing the Chief Moment Officers*, I frame this as the combining of the Bird's Eye View with the Worm's Eye View which allows leaders a much better view of what's really going on. An effective customer knowledge system can start with a commitment to regular gathering of frontline insights and a commitment to co-creation. In addition to improving customer knowledge for improved ease, when frontline staff, (who often feel disconnected from the company leaders and purpose) are regularly involved in designing or refining customer experiences, they feel more important. Co-creation sessions where staff work with leaders sharing their knowledge about real opportunities to make business easier is a great option for happier customers and more engaged staff. Some of the best ways to tap into these invaluable insights include:

1. Company-wide customer feedback repository where anyone can simply log in and share observations or insights.

2. Regular co-creation workshops with frontline staff from a variety of customer facing jobs. Often these staff members aren't used to being brought into strategy development sessions and it helps to begin these sessions with a high-level explanation of the importance of exceptional customer experiences and the importance of every staff member's view. An effective way I've found to help frontline staff feel well prepared and comfortable sharing in settings they may not be used to is to ask, "Can you share any odd, funny or weird customer requests you've seen?" I've found that whether I'm talking to a parking attendant, delivery staff, housekeepers or call center agents, they all have rich answers to this question. Sometimes you'll find issues of low significance, but I've also uncovered serious customer service issues from these exchanges.

Once you establish a culture where frontline staff see they have influence on company decisions and customer experience enhancement you will benefit from having a more engaged workforce motivated to delight customers.

3. Another knowledge capture approach is informal leader rounding. Having key members of management and the c-suite committed to regular visits with the frontline staff offers a few benefits. First, this is a way to hear what customers issues may be right from the source, those who are spend time with customers day in and day out. Next, leaders are more visible, and staff feel more important when they have the opportunity to connect and share their observations with those in charge. Leaders who may have been far removed from the customer action and the state customer ease for many years can begin to regularly refresh their perspectives on how the business is moving forward, or not, through regular informal rounding. Vocera is a company that assists teams in healthcare, hospitality, education, retail, and others with

rounding support solutions for improved collaboration and communication. Their website champions rounding to "proactively identify gaps and deploy improvement".

There are many reasons being easy can be hard for companies to bake into operations and protect long-term. Best-selling business author Joseph Michelli shared his summary of how businesses can lose sight of the importance of effortless experiences, "For me the best customer experience question a leader can ask on a daily basis is, 'how can we make this easier for those we serve? At the same time, we have to think about the ecosystem. That's where another important question comes into play, 'How do I ensure I don't overcomplicate service delivery so our team can be consistent in reducing customer effort?" As your teams strive to grow revenue and customer loyalty, consider questions like those Joseph formed as the foundation of a deliberate customer effort strategy.

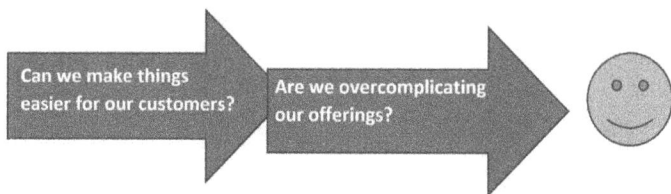

Can we make things easier for our customers?

Are we overcomplicating our offerings?

"Making things easy is hard."

TED NELSON

"The sole reason we are in business
is to make life less difficult for our
clients."

MATT ODGERS

CHAPTER

3

EASY-OLOGY:
Easy Steps for an Easy Strategy

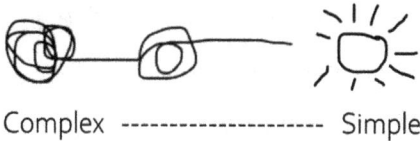

Complex ---------------------- Simple

EASE-OLOGY IS MY SHORTHAND term for the study and application of the power of ease in any business. It's a discipline that moves customer interactions from complex to simple. Every company should consider internal easy-ology studies to strengthen the culture and sustain customer delight and loyalty. Here I propose a formula to advance the current state of easyness in any organization:

Customer Effort Exploration + Customer Aligned Operations= EASE

This simple equation can be applied to any type of offering. C-suite support is crucial since the systems that have made it difficult for customers to do business with you are likely tied to years of well-intentioned decisions and resource allocation. Improvement isn't likely to happen by the push of an Easy button and changes to policies, procedures and systems will need to be seen as part of an overall growth and retention strategy.

As you prepare to build an effective easy strategy, consider pursuing these enhancements: **Extreme Listening, Exploration of Customer Choice, Effort Assessment, Aligned Leaders' Voice and Customer Aligned Operations.**

1. Extreme Listening:

The first step in examining current customer effort involves what I call EXTREME LISTENING. This involves an integrated approach to gathering customer feedback, needs and desires through as many channels as possible. Many companies integrate this invaluable information through customer experience management software systems. Whether you have the depth and funds to automate real-time collection of insights or you have home-grown systems in place, to establish less friction as a core value, you must commit to EXTREME LISTENING. To begin the process, do an inventory of all the ways you gather customer insights and preferences and how well this information is shared internally for effective response. A dedicated team of diverse thinkers in your company should dive in to identify gaps and likely improvements. Or, for a fresh perspective you may contract with consultants to do the assessment. As mentioned in the previous chapter, deliberate systems to gather customer insights from frontline staff should be included in a comprehensive listening strategy. The staff who interact online, in person or on the phone with customers have invaluable knowledge that is too often not leveraged. Once listening has been optimized, and insights are well shared, including what customers say vs. what they do, a valuable next step is to compare those findings to how competitors perform to gain a better understanding of specific customer choice factors.

2. Exploring Customer Choice

In the book, *Grow by Focusing on What Matters,* University of Notre Dame Professor Joe Urbany developed a model that seeks to "explore and exploit new growth opportunities through deep understanding of customers' unmet needs". His model grew to the founding of Vennli, a research company that helps companies focus on customer choice to identify typically hidden insights that can differentiate an offering in the marketplace**.** Griffin Eaton, Vennli Vice President explained, "The moment of truth in any business is when the customer CHOOSES to make the purchase whatever that may be. Many companies have missed the importance of understanding "choice", so they've missed opportunities to positively influence customer choice. We see ease as a key driver of choice". Vennli teams have created a model to look at customer choice by concurrently investigating three important perspectives:

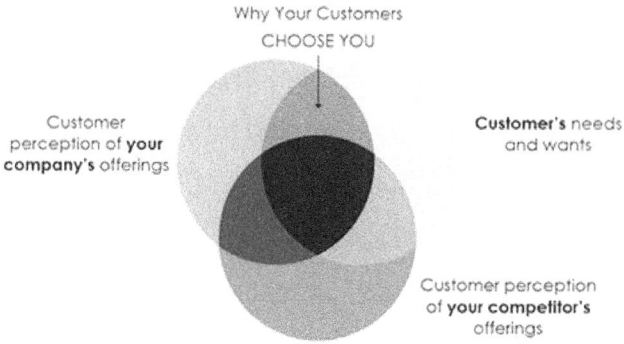

Why Your Customers
CHOOSE YOU

Customer
perception of **your
company's** offerings

Customer's needs
and wants

Customer perception
of **your competitor's**
offerings

Graphic used with Permission ©2008 Vennli

This examination of customer choice helps identify customer perceptions of the experience doing business with your company, their perceptions of doing business with competitors, and then compares those drivers to what is most important to customers. More and more Ease or Simplicity is a priority need and desire across the board.

3. Effort Assessment

Unnecessary customer effort involves points of friction that should be constantly assessed. Some points of friction are deal breakers and can even lead to legal action and others are just annoyances. I like to look for unnecessary effort or friction by initially examining the customer experience at all the front doors of an organization including:

- The digital front door and how easy it is to learn about and purchase offerings
- The physical front door and how easy it is to get in, get what's for sale and get out
- The phone front door and how easy it is to reach the right people, an actual person and conduct business

All entry points should be intuitive, accurate, user-friendly, secure, and flexible to reduce effort whenever possible.

Another way to better understand friction issues comes from a review by a customer relationship management expert who identifies six types of effort customers may face. Emmanuel Richard, CEO of Extens-Consulting a customer experience group headquartered in France has adapted industry thinking to create the *6 Dimensions of Ease*. His 2015 white-paper "Forget Effort, Choose Ease" advises that a focus on ease instead of effort can dramatically change the company's alignment with customers. Emmanuel's philosophy after working with B to B and B to C customers for many years is, "We see customer ease as the required first step for any customer experience strategy development in any industry. Once we explore the 6 Dimensions of Ease in a company, a more robust strategy will be more effective long term". Emmanuel adapted an intriguing term typically applied in the fields of science and engineering that can apply to almost any organization: Customer Simplexity: the need to take what is surely a complex system and make it simple for those who desire to interact and support the system. Scientist Bruce Schiff defined Simplexity as "the process by which nature strives towards simple ends by complex means." Emmanuel and his team at Extens-Consulting work with many industries to review the state of Customer Simplexity as a new way companies can pursue customer effort reduction and focus on the simple ends desired by customers.

Emmanuel's 6 Dimensions of Ease that frame undesirable amounts of customer effort are:

1. *Understanding*: the level of mental energy and intelligent quotient that must be mobilized to get the meaning of a word, a sentence, a text given by a physician, a nurse, an insurer

2. *Navigation*: the different steps to be taken to handle a request such as an appointment with a physician, a dental program, a medical transportation, a refund of medical cost

3. *Interpersonal*: the ease of communicating with one's interlocutor, a nurse, a clinical assistant, a physician, a pharmacist

4. *Physical*: the physical energy that must be deployed such as standing for too long, listening if impaired hearing, reading if impaired vision

5. *Time:* the perception of time at the different stages of the journey such as waiting at the doctor's office, queuing at the hospital's reception, scheduling an appointment

6. *Financial:* gains or spending incurred to obtain satisfaction, such as taking one hour or a half day off, paying parking or going by foot, sending information by email or stamped letter

The concept of measuring customer effort is new to many organizations however something known as the Customer Effort Score was developed in 2010 by the Corporate Executive Board (CEB Global, now Gartner) when research indicated that "effort" is a key driver of customer loyalty. In the 2013 book, *The Effortless Experience* by Matthew Dixon, Nick Toman and Rich Delisi, they shared that "96% of customers with a high-effort service interaction become more disloyal compared to just 9% who have a low-effort experience."

Customer effort scores can assess the ease of customer interactions or resolution of problems so that staff can identify opportunities to improve systems to reliably improve the experience. In the original model, the Customer Effort Score ranges from 0-100. Your CES is the total number of customers who agree that their interaction was easy (rating of 4 or 5) divided by the total number of responses. As of this writing, the consulting group Delighted.com allows companies to survey up to 250 customers for free with their Customer Effort Survey. Customer Effort Score approaches typically involves a single question and scoring with one of these survey types:

A Likert Scale: a 1 to 7 or 1 to 5 scale with 1 representing the highest level of disagreement (Strongly agree to Strongly disagree) with the statement: Was it easy to get an appointment with your physician?

1-10 Scale: with 1 being the best score indicating lowest effort and great ease and 10 being highest effort or great difficulty for questions such as: How much effort was required to make your purchase?

1-5 Scale: with 1 indicating very difficult and 5 indicating very easy for questions such as: How easy was it to get answers to your questions?

Happy/Sad Faces: using three simple face illustrations of happy, sad, and neutral for questions such as: How easy was it for you to return your merchandise?

4. Aligned Leader's Voice

Businesses certainly are never launched expecting to make things difficult for their cherished customers. As covered in previous chapters, there are many issues that allow this to happen. One key consideration in the development of Ease as a strategic imperative is that the owners or C-suite of an organization must be aligned in understanding the power of ease and clearly establish ease as a promise and expectation. In the book, *The Leader's Voice*, Boyd Clark, and Ron Crossland explored the importance of companies nurturing an "understandable vision" so that the entire organization knows what is expected, what is valued and what contributes to success. In many of my client engagements assessing the current state of customer experience strategy, I interview the senior leadership members individually to compare their views of the customer and their views of customer experience strategy tied to operations. It is common to find that the various leaders have vastly different views of how things are working, what they believe is going well and what drives exceptional experiences. After interviewing 10 leaders and walking away with 6 different views of how to please customers while running a viable enterprise, it often becomes clear that an aligned leader's voice is missing.

When leaders are not aligned around business priorities, it's no surprise that teams are confused about what's important. This confusion leads to inconsistency, wasted time and effort and most importantly, an unreliable or misaligned customer experience. The first step is to build awareness among leaders about how important it is that they get on the same page about driving delightful customer experiences. Once that's established, either by education and consensus building or executive direction, then establishing Ease as the true north in the company can begin. Clarke and Crossland emphasize the need for effective communication of this true north as the key to directing teams to get on board. They discussed three core aspects to this communication that enhance understanding and adoption of new habits. The Leader's Voice model recommends that leaders incorporate "Facts, Emotions and Symbols" when preparing the workforce to embrace company goals and aspirations. Applying all three approaches helps to build understanding and recollection so that teams are aligned to the vision and how they should contribute to what's important. When leaders are aligned and that alignment is well communicated, the chances for a high performing organization are great. Every organization should clearly communicate that making it as easy as humanly possible for customers to interact and transact is a core value. Here's a simple example of how to communicate using the F.E.S. model in an imaginary call center operation:

Fact: When customers are put on hold in our call center for more than 19 minutes over 70% abandon the call and of that group only 30% call back. This inability to connect with us in a timely fashion is contributing to lost revenue.

Emotions: If we are unable to respond to callers in a timely fashion the domino effect of lost revenue has a direct cumulative effect on the growth of the company, the ability to fund positions and bonuses and ultimately puts every job in the company at risk.

Symbols: If we ignore the call abandonment issue and the negative impact it has on customer experience and preference, it's as if we have our heads in the sand and a hurricane is approaching. We will be up to date on the properties of the sand, but it won't matter when the hurricane arrives to blow us and the sand away.

This example of applying Facts, Emotions and Symbols illustrates the power of incorporating different perspectives to motivate teams. Using all three frameworks helps to create a compelling case for reliably improved behaviors and systems.

5. Customer Aligned Operations

Unfortunately, we've all seen businesses get our attention with slick promises of awesome and easy experiences only to find out they can't deliver on the promise. Jim Gilmore, co-author of the ground-breaking book, *The Experience Economy* teaches leaders around the world how to better align operations to stage exceptional experiences. On a recent webinar he shared a story about a friend who was a frequent traveler who had frequent issues with hotel accommodations. His friend declared he wished he could "*check into the hotel ad, not the hotel*". This misalignment between what a company promises and what customers actually experience is all too common and a lack of attention to required effort is often the cause. Being easy to do business with must be thoughtfully designed into every point along a customer journey. Priorities such as payment systems, product displays, call centers, mobile apps, return policies, hours of operation, websites are always designed to manage costs, ensure regulatory compliance and efficiency. In today's customer care and experience economy, low customer effort must be thoughtfully designed in as well.

Another compelling case for aligning operations comes from business thought leader Tom Peters who shared his *Future Shape of the Winner* model in 2003. I was certified in this model with Tom's team who outlined three axes that must stay in balance for a company to maintain solid customer satisfaction, strong revenue, and strong reputation. The *Future Shape of the Winner* approach has talent at the center (since all we do depends upon who we recruit and retain within the organization). Next there are three priority axes that need to stay in balance: Ambition must be aligned with Performance, Architecture (Structure & Systems) must be aligned with Execution and lastly, the key for customer satisfaction… Brand must be aligned with Experience. This last axis requires that companies make brand promises clear to every member of the staff so that customers experience what was promised.

Placing customer effort at the center of decision-making and the way offerings are designed and launched can be as simple as adding a customer ease impact review as a requirement for funding. This added step should examine intended and potential unintended impact of likely effort. Here are a few examples of customer-centered perks that would certainly impact operations decisions:

All-inclusive Anything: Aging expert, Anthony Cirillo shared his delight with a lawn care company. He is a devoted customer since they offer all services without "nickel and dime-ing" him to death. They have fair all-inclusive pricing for weeding, mowing, fertilizing, debris removal all designed so that customers don't have to think about the lawn all season. If an all-inclusive model were applied to your business, how would that impact staffing, pricing, marketing, and supply management decisions?

24-Hour Access: Hospitals, nursing homes and rehab centers have visitor policies primarily to maintain security and restfulness for patients. One way these operations can align with customer desires is to make it easy for friends and family to be with their loved ones during times that can be very lonely and scary. Many hospitals have turned the visitation control paradigm upside down by allowing 24-hour access and even sleep-along policies to enhance the patient experience. This presents a complex set of operations changes yet can turn a mediocre experience into a delightful one. Unfortunately, these customer delighting policies had to be halted as the Covid 19 pandemic impacted almost everything about resident or patient visitation. No matter what business you're in, where might 24-hour access enhance the customer experience?

Self-select Appointments: this may be difficult to sustain but allowing customers to tell you a convenient time for a service call is one of the best easy strategies of all. Imagine a car dealership that asks you when you'd like to bring your car in for an oil change and imagine if they offered evening and weekend options. Again, there are surely many issues to be addressed to provide flexible scheduling, but it's a sure path to raving fans. In addition to personalized scheduling, many car dealerships strive to offer an easier purchasing experience by arranging for state registration paperwork to be completed onsite or delivering cars to your home. When leadership teams begin with a desire to make life easy for customers, it may be more complicated to resource, but it can be a competitive game changer. Think about possible self-select options that could be added to your offerings.

Jargon Hunting: The use of jargon can often cause confusion, certainly for new customers. It helps to

periodically review customer facing materials to eliminate jargon that can be misleading and complicate
an otherwise easy interaction. When customers don't
understand the language needed to do business
with a company, they feel lost and removing jargon
is an easy cure. Consider assigning a jargon hunting
team to seek and destroy unnecessary jargon in your
organization.

First Contact Resolution: This customer relationship
management goal is typically applied in call centers. Companies that aspire to achieve first contact
resolution strive to operate in a manner that when
customers reach out, no follow-up is necessary. This
commitment to meeting needs and resolving issues
with one call, one visit, one email or one chat requires
extensive training and reliable information systems.
It also requires that front-line staff have a span of
authority that allows prompt guidance and resolution. This customer ease strategy is a foundation for
an effective path to long-term customer preference
and satisfaction. Investigate how many first contact
resolution systems exist in your company.

⛵ Path Clearing Exercise #5:
Framing your Easy Strategy

As a team, review one word at a time to explore how and when your organization lives up to the ease implications for your customers:

Quick	Knowledgeable
Relevant	Clear
Guided	Seamless
Straightforward	Painless
Well-designed	Careful
Thoughtful	Reasonable
Carefree	Accessible
Simple	Customized
Effortless	Not repetitive
Proficient	Well connected
Uncomplicated	Flexible
Comfortable	Anticipatory
On time	Obstacles removed

⛵ Path Clearing Exercise #6

How NOT to frame customer experiences:

We've all had the experience where we couldn't believe how difficult it was to do business with a business. Sometimes it's one step after another that's unbelievably cumbersome or complex and other times it's one aspect such as trying to give them money or trying to have them live up to what they promised. I have been in situations like this and wondered, "how oh how do they stay in business?" These experiences help experience design practitioners define what **NOT** to do. Here are some words that frame an intended or unintended Customer Avoidance Strategy or ***things we should avoid doing so customers don't want to avoid us***!

As with the previous positive framework exercise, take each word and explore where or when it might apply in your organization and how you might stop the madness…

Cumbersome	Complex	Rigid
Incomplete	Awkward	Uninformed
Rude	Unprepared	Inconvenient
Duplicative	Slow	Restricted
Inconsistent	Tedious	Unprepared
Repetitive	Ineffective	Unsafe
Obstacles	Confusing	Late

♨ Path Clearing Exercise #7:

Building an Ease Strategy

Step 1—ALIGN LEADERS AND TEAMS FOR A RENEWED COMMITMENT TO CUSTOMER EASE AS A CORE PROMISE.

Declaring that making life as easy as possible for customers is a company commitment doesn't stop with the making of the declaration. That is the beginning. As with any company-wide priority and associated behaviors, all staff must understand the priority, be willing to support it and have the permission and tools needed to deliver on the promise of ease. Alignment around Ease as a core value will require ongoing communication about

The What: *We want to offer an easiest possible experience for every customer, every day.*

And

The Why: *We understand that every customer has a choice to do business with us or someone else. Since we would always prefer an easy, effortless experience ourselves, and want to be the most preferred solution*

in the marketplace, ease will be at the center of all we do. Include all the benefits for customers, staff, and the organization.

The How: *We will work with one another to continually review how doing business with us is clear, uncompli-cated, quick, accessible, and as effortless as possible.*

Step 2—FRICTION IDENTIFICATION: examine where you make it hard for customers.

 Discover how to reduce friction for customers by reviewing common complaints, interviewing customer-facing staff, and comparing and contrasting your approaches to competitors.

- What is redundant?
- What is slow?
- What is confusing?
- What not automated that could be?
- What can be touch-less?
- What should have remote or digital access?
- What is inflexible?
- What is not available online?

Step 3—EASE IMPROVEMENT: prioritize enhancements to be made:

Workforce Enlightenment: Assess current systems to gather prompt customer feedback directly or through artificial intelligence and how well the voice of the customer is shared and translated throughout the organization.

Preserve and Purge: Determine what is working well to reduce customer effort and any stupid systems to eliminate. Prioritize the pursuit of ease by asking these questions:

What's easy to change and offers high impact for customers? What's easy to improve and offers some impact for customers? What's hard to do yet offers high impact for customers?

This process will allow for some initial wins while building visibility around long-term effort goals.

Active Anticipation: Leveraging the power of proactivity can offer great satisfaction gains by reducing the need for human led transactions or interactions where something simple becomes complicated. Review customer journeys and complaints to identify ways to head off unnecessary steps or contacts. Look for opportunities to proactively send clear information or notifications so customers are well prepared to have their needs met. Customer-facing staff should have keen knowledge of pertinent context at the right time and place to reduce effort and increase loyalty.

⛴ Path Clearing Exercise #8:
Likely Customer Reaction Checklist

Rate your organization on how likely customers are to express the following sentiments:

	Never	Often	Always
I can get what I want when I want it.	☐	☐	☐
When I need them I can reach them.	☐	☐	☐
The deliverables/products I receive are what was expected.	☐	☐	☐
When I have a question, I can get prompt, accurate answers.	☐	☐	☐
When I have a problem, I know who can resolve it.	☐	☐	☐
They make our life easier.	☐	☐	☐

"Out of clutter, find simplicity."

ALBERT EINSTEIN

"Simple can be harder than complex: You have to work hard to get your thinking clean to make it simple. But it's worth it in the end because once you get there, you can move mountains."

STEVE JOBS

Ease in Action

WE ALL HAVE STORIES of times when all doors were opened for us as we prepared to make a purchase. Often our reaction to nearly effortless experiences is to be pleasantly surprised or shocked. Companies that have mastered impressive levels of Ease for customers are typically labeled "disruptors". What does it say about the state of business when making life easier for customers prompts shock and awe? It says we have been distracted and let operations drive too many decisions for too long and the customer experience needs to be reimagined as an operations imperative.

Here is a collection of "exceptionally easy" companies that offer lessons for any industry. Of course, they may not have 100 % satisfied customers for many reasons, however I know them to have demonstrated remarkable levels of *Ease in Action*.

Credit Card Champions

I've written about my favorite credit card company in *Unleashing the Chief Moment Officers* but must explore their customer ease systems once again. The key to Discover Card's customer experience leadership centers upon easy access to a real-live informed person to assist with almost anything.

I've been delighted by the ability to obtain a quick connection and speak with kind and well-prepared customer service agents**.** On one Friday night around 10 pm, I received a text from Discover seeking to confirm my attempt to use my card 400 miles away from where I was. Thankfully, I was able to reach a live agent within 3 rings to report that I was not the one shopping. The agent had my card cancelled and a new card on the way to me within 12 minutes. She assured me I wouldn't have to worry about any bogus charges and empathized with my concern while assuring me all was well and even encouraged me to get a good night's sleep. This almost effortless approach to help me manage the threat of theft offered a sense of ease on so many levels!

Simply Shopping

I am an occasional online shopper but the most consistently easy online retail experience I've had has been with Overstock.com. I can explore inventory for hours and once I'm ready to buy, the Overstock shopping cart experience is wonderfully swift. No re-entering information I have provided before, no time-consuming upselling attempts to slow me down, no digging around for hidden fees. I've also always been impressed with how quickly my items arrive, usually earlier than expected and re-order information is always waiting for me in my account.

Painless Health Caring

Wide adoption of electronic medical records began in the early 2000's with US regulations requiring meaningful use of electronic medical records set for 2014. One of the most consumer-friendly aspect of this medical care innovation is the individual patient portal. These centralized records of medical activity have revolutionized consumer access and management of personal healthcare paths. Healthcare is typically described as one of the most complicated industries to navigate by consumers and the electronic medical record portals allow consumers to make appointments, access test results, communicate with clinicians, research credible medical resources 24 hours a day. Some of the patient portal solutions are offered through health systems while others are stand-alone solutions consumers can build on their own. I have had consistently exceptional experiences with the patient portal, MyChart from Epic Corporation. This extensive solution saves a massive amount of time coordinating care, medications, annual screenings, and ongoing appointments. This customer ease strategy can also save lives when patients have improved ability to stay up to date with preventative care and access medical answers quickly.

Button Activated

As the Staples Easy Button framed the company brand promise, they are actively delivering ease for B2B customers through their StaplesAdvantage.

com program. This customer experience innovation is particularly relevant for small and mid-sized companies and basically makes supply ordering, inventory management and spending review extremely simple. Companies sign up for the program and their supply lists are customized to their needs. They are introduced to a dedicated Account Manager and an order approval system is put in place. Another level of ease is that all deliveries are free. In this case, Staples has made the entire office supply and purchasing department function easier to outsource than ever.

Cool Cars

Used car buying has rarely been described as an easy and delightful experience. Carvana Co-founder Ryan Keeton has stated in interviews that their model has been so dedicated to an easy and exceptional experience that "many customers, especially those in new markets, think Carvana is too good to be true".

At Carvana ease comes to life with the 24-hour access to an inventory of thousands of cars. As customers click on possible vehicles, they have easy access to detailed photos of all sections of the car. Once they choose a car, it can be delivered to their home as soon as the next day or arrangements can be made for pick up at a car vending machine around the country. Carvana paid extra ease attention to the purchase agreement process with software that completes most contracts so that instead of hours of paperwork and financing steps, the actual purchase transaction is often a 10-minute process. The added extraordinary perk on top of this list of conveniences is that Carvana offers an easy seven-day return policy.

Gifting Guidance

Amazon has disrupted the shopping experience for all of us and one of ease factor I most appreciate is Amazon's FIND A GIFT tab. This extensive search engine allows you to select from over 20 categories to explore common and uncommon gifts for the man, woman, child, or teen on your list. Results seem to be never-ending and load quickly and certainly simplifies the gift giving process overall.

Expedited Waiting

Chick fil-A has built demand for their tasty nuggets, salads, and sandwiches for over thirty years. However, when pandemic restrictions on eating in restaurants took over the country, the demand and associated drive through lines at exploded. My experience in 3 different states observing Chick-fil-A respond to the demand and impressive flow of cars at all hours of the day is that leaders did all they could to design a low-effort experience. Despite the long lines, ease was preserved by having added adequate staff to take orders and process credit cards ahead of the order board, clear traffic pattern markings and signs, a special-order expediting system, well prepared professionals at the windows and an easy-to-use app. The Chick fil-A response to takeout demand has been applauded on the internet suggesting that the experts at Chick-fil-A should manage distribution of the Covid vaccine.

Show them the Money

Venmo is a payment app where customer ease drives the entire experience. This disruptive payment service eliminates the complications that come with cash payments and allows us to benefit from social friend networks. People can easily borrow and lend money to anyone no matter where they do their banking. And businesses can make it easier for customers to pay virtually as well. The "paying a bill" experience has more options now beyond just what's in a bank account or adding credit card debt.

Remote Bankers

Tom Peters once said, "banking is necessary, banks are not". This prediction from the early 90's didn't result in the end of bank buildings but certainly banking has changed. A variety of digital banking options has made banking easier. A new example of easy banking is video banking which also had a growth spurt because of the 2020 pandemic. Most banks and credit unions offer this option and customers benefit from new levels of convenience while they maintain a face-to-face relationship with staff at their favorite branch. Notre Dame Federal Credit Union's video banking allowed easy scheduling online and direct communication with a well-informed local branch manager. This very convenient yet personal approach helps instill and maintain trust despite the stress of the pandemic.

Outstanding Ease Offerings

The following are enhancements to customer experiences that can enhance Ease. If the specific offering doesn't apply, consider taking the topic and stretching it to apply in your organization. Play with the possibilities of what the ultimate benefit to your customers might be if you applied these concepts:

Less Effort/Complexity/Friction

1. Click to call- 3 or less clicks
2. Free & easy returns
3. Stay home access replacing in person visits
4. Free return pick-up
5. Automated refill/repurchases
6. Group/family scheduling instead of individual
7. Free childcare while shopping
8. Pre-paid return labels and pick up
9. No questions returns/exchanges 10- All inclusive, well priced packages

More Information:/Preparation

1. Personalized shopping consultation Pre-surgery or pre-purchase Instructions for use
2. Online orientation for new customers
3. Price, product descriptions and benefit shopping comparisons
4. Abundant inventory availability information
5. Clear delivery options

♟ Path Clearing Exercise #9:

Discouraging Customer Ease Checklist

Score your organization or department to gauge where you may be discouraging customers through cumbersome policies:

	We're Easy	We're Hard
1. Customers have control	☐	☐
2. It's easy to learn about us	☐	☐
3. It's easy to gather & hold products	☐	☐
4. Customers can reach us easily	☐	☐
5. Customers can try before buy?	☐	☐
6. Prompt answers to questions	☐	☐
7. Pricing transparency exists	☐	☐
8. Physical safety is assured	☐	☐
9. Purchase process is quick	☐	☐
10. Customization is easy	☐	☐

11. Staff are empowered to delight ☐ ☐

12. Redundant steps are removed ☐ ☐

13. Staff are committed to ease ☐ ☐

14. Customer Insights broadly shared ☐ ☐

15. Customers receive proactive updates ☐ ☐

16. Customers have many choices ☐ ☐

Old Ways to Frame a New Ease Strategy- as teams examine ways to improve customer effort, the application of diverse frameworks can offer new perspectives. Here are some traditional descriptions of Ease to prompt new ways to think about clearing paths for your customers:

1. Strive to be "as easy as pie."

Where did this phrase come from?

Similes give an example of something that is well-known to display a property that can be used to describe another, such as "blue as the sky". Being easy as pie is a common description however, how are pies thought to be easy? A variety of sources conclude that, while not being easy to make, pies are generally thought to be easy to eat. At least, in 19th century America, where this phrase is believed to have originated. There are various mid-19th century US citations point to 'pie' being used to denote pleasantness and ease.

As you hire and prepare staff to represent a promise of ease, it's important that you clearly define the desired behaviors and experiential aspirations. "Easy as pie" may be a bit too vague for staff to connect how they can contribute to the desired customer experience. Be sure to thoughtfully design and explain how all staff members can have influence to create ease for customers. When the steps staff need to take require great effort, extra communication and support will be needed to build commitment to end up with a well baked and effortless customer experience.

2. Flying through the air with the greatest of ease...1868 'The Daring Young Man on the Flying Trapeze'.

Not many of us have taken a turn on a flying trapeze but the image of effort-lessly swaying through the air without a care in the world is another common ease frame-work. Yes, a trapeze is daring, since the ground offers a hard stop, but so is being in business. The example of daring to climb up and get on board and delib-erately pursue a journey with the greatest of ease requires commitment, accountability, enthusiasm, and courage. Consider this metaphor as you establish customer experience standards and push teams to not just make things easier, but to think bigger, take some risks to offer the "greatest of ease!"

3. Easy Street

Miriam-Webster.com defines "easy street" as a situation with no worries or one of wealth and ease. Protecting customers from all sorts of worries is a great way to reframe operations and interactions with customers. Develop a No Worries List to review with leaders and frontline staff. You can periodically survey customers to ask- What aspects of doing business with us causes you concern or worry? Specific areas to dig deeper on may include: Worries about costs, timeliness, accuracy, safety, effectiveness, support, ethics, repairs, cleanliness, privacy, reliability and access to answers, systems, human guidance.

4. At ease troops…

This is a common phrase in tv shows and movies when a military leader directs the troops to be "at ease". What does "at ease" mean? The general definition I found was that at ease is *a less formal, less rigid relaxed position in the military. The phrase is often used as a command for troops standing at attention to shift to a relaxed stance.*

As you prepare the workforce to do their best, consider adding the expectation that all staff are to help all customers be "at ease". Of course, having a workforce of high performers requires them being "at ease" with what they need to do for customers. Well prepared and aligned teams with the tools they need to do the job have less stress around their daily responsibilities and help make work easier for your staff. How might you do a better job helping your staff be at ease and well prepared so they can help customers be at ease?

5. Smooth Sailing and Smooth as Silk.

The idiom, *Smooth Sailing* was noted over a century ago and was associated to an easy boat trip free from rough waters. We now apply this regularly to many aspects of life including how hard it may be to purchase or use goods or services. This option for imagining a customer effort strategy focuses on the ability to progress or advance without rough waters or barriers. Think about how well your teams work to improve a customer's ability to progress to purchase or progress for repeat purchases and endorsement.

The frequently used phrase Smooth as Silk refers to the slippery nature of silk cloth. The phrase describes a promise of a lack of impediments, hinderances or obstacles. Customers will have a more difficult time becoming and remaining customers when impediments are allowed to live in your company. As you examine your customer journeys identify what's smooth as silk and what tends to hinder a silky-smooth experience.

6. It's a Breeze

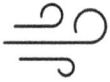

The ultimate description of a great customer experience is when customers say, "it was a breeze!" The last of our 10 exercises can help teams align people and systems to be worthy of this endorsement.

⛵ Path Clearing Exercise #10:
Check Your Breeze Scale

IT'S A BREEZE… a simple and carefree experience, easy accomplishment.

The Customer Effort Breeze Scale™

▼   ▼   ▼   ▼

It's a Breeze	It's Tolerable	It's Too Hard	It's Ridiculous
Light Air	*Gentle Breeze*	*Moderate Breeze*	*Gusts & Gales*

The Customer Experience Is:

Pleasant Refreshing	Annoying Irritating	Frustrating Upsetting	Destructive Exasperating

What Customers Do:

Stay Loyal	Acclimate	Complain	Exit

What Companies Should Do:

Maintain	Investigate	Intervene	Sound Alarm

One way to frame the delivery of exceptionally effort-less experiences is to strive for customers to say, **"That was a breeze!"** Using the imagery around breezes and the definition of something being easy, this scale can be used to measure your systems, com-munications, and accessibility for customers to have a delightful, easy experience.

The Beaufort Wind Scale guides weather experts on the type and impact of winds in our world. This metaphor offers a fresh look at business decisions and the potential impact on customer ease. Ask your teams, how far are we from making life a breeze for our customers? Where are we on the scale?

Light Air Breeze—in the atmosphere this is a comforting, refreshing and overall a pleasant experience with little or no disruption in the environment. In business this is a perfect goal for your customers. How do you comfort your customers and offer little or no disruption, just prompt access to meeting their needs?

Gentle Breeze—in nature, this breeze can be felt on the skin and prompt some rustling of leaves but is typically a pleasant experience. In business, this offers little or no friction for your customers is usually tolerated well without driving customers to a competitor. This should be the phase where customers learn how to navigate working with you to have their needs met and once that step is completed, it should all be a breeze.

Moderate Breeze—here we see dust and leaves raise up and trees sway, flags begin to extend. When customers face this level of complication or frustration, there's motivation for customers to consider shopping somewhere else and dissatisfaction is expressed through multiple channels and many will leave.

Strong Breeze/Gales—these conditions prompt weather alerts and large branches are moving and breaking, resistance is felt on your face, destruction can occur. When your business presents this level of frustration the entire customer relationship can break down leading to wide dissatisfaction, no demand, closures or even lawsuits. If your operations force customers to face a windstorm of complications, broken promises, inefficiencies, redundancies, and delays, it's time to re-align to be "It's a Breeze-worthy". A "dangerous conditions" alert needs to be shared so your organization does not get blown away by the competition!

"When you raise the convenience bar, you create the next level of amazing customer experience."

Shep Hyken

"Few things generate more goodwill and repeat business than being effortless to deal with."

Matt Watkinson

Summary

BUILDING A VIABLE BUSINESS requires attracting and retaining customers. To sustain this, the most basic commitment must be to *clear a path for customers in every way possible*, so they are not lost in a world of roadblocks that aren't worth navigating.

Every business has unintentionally made life difficult for customers at some point. Things like paperwork that takes longer to complete than the actual visit with the doctor, non-existent contact numbers on a website, missing instructions on what not to do before opening a box, use of acronyms that only your team understands, frontline staff who have inadequate training or authority to fix a problem, complex password protocols, no overflow seating in a waiting room or renewal systems that forget a customer is an existing customer… all of these situations are customer experience system failures. It's hard to be easy all of the time, but a focus on continually identifying and improving what's difficult is what smart companies do well.

All businesses can benefit from an ongoing assessment of effort and ease realities. There can be many cultural, operations and competitive forces that contribute to unnecessary levels of complexity. The solution is the deliberate pursuit of a *Customer Ease Strategy* as an ongoing leadership priority to increase the odds for long-term simplicity. The design of effortless customer experiences won't just happen. Consider these next steps:

- Leaders declaring Ease as a top priority is the first step to clearing all paths for customers.
- Assessment of the current state to identify what's easy and what's hard is the next important step toward reliable performance. This stage should include friction mapping to identify what is repetitive, what's unclear and any dead-ends customers face when interacting with staff, systems, and facilities.

- Preparing the workforce to embrace a commitment to Ease will likely take the longest amount of time but ultimately will drive a low customer effort culture to drive growth and loyalty. This involves continual training and awareness building.

Of course, there are many views of what's most important for customers, but my view is that if an enterprise is not first easy to find or engage with, the other aspects of an offering just may not matter. An Ease Strategy influences operations, compliance, marketing, sales, and resource decision-making with the likely customer effort in mind.

It should be common business sense that respecting the time of customers, communicating clearly, being transparent and proactive, maintaining systems to capture and share knowledge to better anticipate needs and committing to simplification helps drive growth. When a company achieves reliable Ease, customer satisfaction and enthusiastic endorsements won't be far behind. Establishing your company as the easiest to access can directly drive new revenue since some will be willing to pay more to enjoy a less complex or tedious experience.

Without a commitment to low customer effort, businesses run the risk of alienating customers and the opportunity to respond and repair the relationship may never come. There may be some accommodations or perks you can offer to distract customers from how hard you are to do business with, but that is likely a short-term strategy. Long-term customer loyalty requires authentic low friction commitments. Yes, it can be *hard to be easy* but hopefully the concepts presented here will prompt teams to explore enhancements to become reliably easy very soon.

"Simplicity boils down to two steps: Identify the essential. Eliminate the rest."

LEO BABAUTA

"Complexity is the enemy of execution. "

TONY ROBERTS

"Simplicity is a sign of truth and a criterion of beauty. Complexity can be a way of hiding the truth."

Helena Rubinstein

"At minimum, [a streamlined retail experience] must be error-free and smooth, otherwise your customers *will* notice. And most of the time, they won›t say anything about it — they'll just shop somewhere else next time around."

Jessica Thiele, marketing manager, VL OMNI

"Everything is easier said than done. Wanting something is easy. Saying something is easy. The challenge and the reward are in the doing."

STEVE MARABOLI

"Digital is taking proximity/convenience retailing to a new level of customer centricity. There is nothing more convenient than a store in your pocket or in your handbag."

PATRICK DODD, PRESIDENT, GLOBAL RETAILER, NIELSEN.

"The idea is that companies put the least amount of thought into self-service. They make customers do a cirque de soleil act to solve a problem."

Blake Morgan

"Consumers are always looking for an easier way to do and get more."

TextRequest.com

"Make It Effortlessly Swift - deliver a customer experience with ease. It's one way Zappos turns customers into raving fans."

Joseph Michelli

Diane Serbin Hopkins

Diane Serbin Hopkins

is the mother of Benjamin Serbin Stover and a national thought leader on customer experience and innovation strategy. She's the author of the book *Unleashing the Chief Moment Officers* and co-author of *Advice from a Patient* and *Wake Up and Smell the Innovation*. She has been described as a pioneer in reinventing the role of a marketer in connecting brand to experience. She was one of the first Chief Experience Officers and Chief Innovation Officers in the US healthcare industry. Diane received the 2012 Customer Experience Innovation Award from the Customer Experience Professionals Association, the Experience Management Achievement Award from Strategic Horizons, the Professional Excellence Award and Young Marketer Award from the Society for Health Care Strategy and Market Development.

She is a national speaker on Innovation Culture and Customer and Patient Experience Strategy. Diane was a founding faculty member at the University of Notre Dame Innovation Mentor Program, Executive Director of the Medline Patient Experience and Innovation Institute, Adjunct Faculty at the Pennsylvania College of Health Science and a frequent speaker at

Beckers Healthcare Roundtable and the Cleveland Clinic Empathy and Innovation Conferences. Diane and her team at the Healthworks Kids' Museum were featured in the PBS special Re-Imagine Business Excellence with Tom Peters.

As CEO of ExPeers she's consulted and trained customer experience coaches throughout the US and Europe and offers special focus on the importance of safety within the customer experience, how innovative problem-solving impacts customer experience and the many benefits of co-creation in customer experience design. You can reach out to Diane at www.expeers.net

"Why in the world would any organization allow it's people, procedures or policies to impede the ability for customers to be customers? Because it's hard to be easy."

Diane Serbin Hopkins

www.ingramcontent.com/pod-product-compliance
Lightning Source LLC
Chambersburg PA
CBHW032246210326
41458CB00083B/6776/J

* 9 7 8 1 9 5 5 7 5 0 1 0 3 *